PLAN A
LIFE
YOU LOVE
JOURNAL

A WOMEN'S GUIDE TO HEALTH, WEALTH AND HAPPINESS WITHOUT LIMITATIONS

HANNA OLIVAS
LENA KHAIS | SYLVIA BECKER-HILL | TRISH GLEASON
PRUDENCE HATCHETT

ISBN: 978-1-968061-72-2

Table of Contents

Hanna Olivas

Founder and CEO of SHE RISES STUDIOS

https://www.linkedin.com/company/she-rises-studios/
https://www.facebook.com/sherisesstudios
https://www.instagram.com/sherisesstudios_llc/
www.SheRisesStudios.com

Author, Speaker, and Founder. Hanna was born and raised in Las Vegas, Nevada, and has paved her way to becoming one of the most influential women of 2022. Hanna is the co-founder of She Rises Studios and the founder of the Brave & Beautiful Blood Cancer Foundation. Her journey started in 2017 when she was first diagnosed with Multiple Myeloma, an incurable blood cancer. Now more than ever, her focus is to empower other women to become leaders because The Future is Female. She is currently traveling and speaking publicly to women to educate them on entrepreneurship, leadership, and owning the female power within.

Plan A Life You Love...

A JOURNEY WITHIN

A Message From the Author — Hanna Olivas, Creator of Plan a Life You Love™

This journal isn't just paper and prompts.
It's a mirror.
A reminder.
A declaration.
That you are not here to simply exist—you are here to live.

To rise boldly.
To take up space.
To rewrite the rules that told you to settle, shrink, or wait.

I created Plan a Life You Love during a time when I needed to remember who I was... and more importantly, who I was becoming.
This isn't about perfection.
It's about permission—to grow, to heal, to cry, to laugh, to fail forward, to start over... again and again if needed. So write like
your future depends on it.

Dream like no one's watching.
And plan a life so powerful, so joyful, so unapologetically YOU—
that the world has no choice but to take notice.

Let this be your beginning.
Not someday.
Not maybe.
Now.

**HANNA OLIVAS - THE RESILIENCE MAVEN™ | AUTHOR, MOTHER, FIGHTER,
CREATOR OF SHECONOMY™**

Rooted in Purpose

This is where your journey begins — with intention. Living a life you love starts by understanding who you truly are and why you're here. This section invites you to dig deep into your core values, passions, and purpose. It's not about having all the answers but about tuning into the inner whispers that guide your soul. You'll begin planting the seeds of a life that feels deeply meaningful.

- What does a "life I love" look like in vivid detail?

- What brings me joy without external validation?

- What values do I want my life to reflect?

- When do I feel most aligned with my purpose?

_____

_____

_____

_____

_____

_____

_____

_____

_____

_____

_____

Purpose isn't found, it's remembered — it lives quietly within you, waiting to be awakened.

Rooted in Purpose

Purpose isn't found, it's remembered — it lives quietly within you, waiting to be awakened.

The Power of Vision

Before you can live a life you love, you must dare to imagine it. This section helps you cast a bold vision for your future — one shaped by your dreams, not your doubts. Here, you'll give yourself permission to dream without limits and to craft a vision that excites your spirit. You'll begin to see your future with clarity and conviction.

- If there were no limits, what would I be doing right now?

- What does "living out loud" mean to me personally?

- What are 3 dreams I've been afraid to speak out loud?

- Create a vision board or describe your dream life in words.

_____
_____
_____
_____
_____
_____
_____
_____
_____
_____
_____

Your dreams are not too big — they're just waiting for you to believe in them as fiercely as they believe in you.

The Power of Vision

Your dreams are not too big — they're just waiting for you to believe in them as fiercely as they believe in you.

From Fear to Freedom

Transformation demands courage. This section invites you to identify and face the fears, limiting beliefs, and past wounds that have kept you stuck or small. With compassion and honesty, you'll begin to rewrite your inner narrative and free yourself from patterns that no longer serve you. Healing becomes the gateway to your personal liberation.

- What fear is currently holding me back from living fully?

- Write a letter to your past self thanking them for their resilience.

- What limiting beliefs am I ready to release?

- Recall a challenge you overcame. What did it teach you?

_____

_____

_____

_____

_____

_____

_____

_____

_____

_____

_____

_____

Fear may visit, but it doesn't get to unpack. You are meant to live in freedom.

From Fear to Freedom

Fear may visit, but it doesn't get to unpack. You are meant to live in freedom.

Passion & Career Alignment

Work should feel like an extension of your purpose — not just a paycheck. This section helps you reflect on your current career or calling, and whether it lights you up or leaves you depleted. It's an opportunity to explore the intersection of passion, talent, and impact — so you can pursue work that fuels your joy and adds value to the world.

- What kind of work would I do for free because I love it so much?

- What skills or passions do I want to explore or revive?

- Is my current career path aligned with my values and passions?

- What does "success" look like to me?

_____
_____
_____
_____
_____
_____
_____
_____
_____
_____
_____

Do what sets your soul on fire — The world needs your light, not your burnout.

Passion & Career Alignment

Do what sets your soul on fire — The world needs your light, not your burnout.

Sacred Self-Care

Loving yourself isn't selfish — it's essential. In this section, you'll explore how you care for your physical, emotional, mental, and spiritual well-being. You'll define what self-love means on your own terms and reflect on the ways you can nurture yourself consistently. Because when your cup is full, you can live — and give — from overflow.

- How do I show myself love and compassion?

- What drains me, and how can I release it?

- What makes me feel safe, seen, and supported?

- Design your ideal "self-love day." What would you do?

_____

_____

_____

_____

_____

_____

_____

_____

_____

_____

_____

_____

You are not a machine. Rest is your right. Self care is your sacred return to self.

Sacred Self-Care

You are not a machine. Rest is your right. Self-care is your sacred return to self.

Meaningful Connections

Date:
_____

Relationships shape the quality of our lives. This section focuses on cultivating connections that are authentic, nourishing, and aligned. You'll reflect on the people you surround yourself with, the kind of relationships you want to build, and how to show up more fully in love, friendship, and community — starting with the relationship you have with yourself.

- Who are the people that make me feel alive and accepted?

- What kind of relationships am I calling into my life?

- Where am I holding back from authentic connection?

- How can I be more present with the people I love?

_____
_____
_____
_____
_____
_____
_____
_____
_____
_____
_____

You are worthy of relationships that feel like home — soft, strong, and soul-nourishing.

Meaningful Connections

You are worthy of relationships that feel like home
— soft, strong, and soul-nourishing.

Living Out Loud

This is where you step into the spotlight of your own life — unapologetically. Living out loud means showing up as your true self, honoring your voice, and expressing your truth with courage. This section helps you embody authenticity and claim your power so you can live boldly, fully, and without regret.

- Where in my life am I playing small?

- What does being unapologetically me look like?

- How can I express my truth more boldly this week?

- What legacy do I want to leave behind?

_____
_____
_____
_____
_____
_____
_____
_____
_____
_____
_____
_____

This is your life — speak it, live it, and wear it boldly. There's no one else like you.

Living Out Loud

_____
_____
_____
_____
_____
_____
_____
_____
_____
_____
_____
_____
_____
_____
_____
_____
_____
_____
_____
_____
_____

This is your life — speak it, live it, and wear it boldly. There's no one else like you.

Gratitude & Growth

Gratitude turns what you have into enough, and growth transforms who you are into who you're becoming. This section helps you pause, reflect, and celebrate your journey. You'll acknowledge both the beauty and the lessons, appreciating how far you've come — and how every step, even the hard ones, shaped your evolution.

- List 5 things you're deeply grateful for right now.

- What lesson am I learning in this season of life?

- Reflect on how far you've come in the past year.

- Who or what helped you grow in unexpected ways?

Growth isn't always loud. Sometimes, it's in the quiet gratitude of simply showing up.

Gratitude & Growth

Growth isn't always loud. Sometimes, it's in the quiet gratitude of simply showing up.

Inspired Action

Clarity means little without action. This section bridges dreaming and doing. You'll commit to bold, intentional steps toward your vision and purpose — no more waiting, overthinking, or seeking permission. Whether it's a small act of courage or a major life decision, you're invited to move forward in faith and momentum.

- What's one small step I can take today toward a life I love?

- What will I commit to this week that supports my vision?

- Where can I replace procrastination with empowered action?

- Set a 30-day intention. What do you want to manifest or change?

_____

_____

_____

_____

_____

_____

_____

_____

_____

_____

_____

_____

Don't wait for perfect — move now. Clarity
follows motion, not the other way around.

Inspired Action

_____
_____
_____
_____
_____
_____
_____
_____
_____
_____
_____
_____
_____
_____
_____
_____
_____
_____
_____
_____
_____

Don't wait for perfect — move now. Clarity follows motion, not the other way around.

Reflection & Celebration

Every journey deserves a moment of pause, reflection, and celebration. In this final section, you'll honor your growth, your breakthroughs, and your bravery. You'll witness your own transformation and recognize the beauty of the life you're now creating — a life you love, lived out loud, with intention, joy, and purpose.

- What am I most proud of in my journey so far?

- How have I begun to live more out loud?

- What would I tell someone just starting this journey?

- Celebrate yourself: Write a love letter to your future self.

_____

_____

_____

_____

_____

_____

_____

_____

_____

_____

_____

You made it here — not by chance, but by courage. Celebrate wildly. You are becoming."

Reflection & Celebration

You made it here — not by chance, but by courage. Celebrate wildly. You are becoming."

Lena Khais

Founder and CEO of Atlas Paradigm
Manifestation Coach

https://bit.ly/LenaKhais
https://www.facebook.com/lifebydesignforbusinesswomen
https://bit.ly/Lena_Khais
www.atlas-paradigm.com

Lena Khais is a seasoned mindset coach dedicated to guiding individuals on transformative journeys by demystifying manifestation. With a passion for unlocking the mind's potential, Lena empowers people to attract the life they authentically desire. Her unique coaching approach blends neuroscience, spirituality, and humor, creating an engaging and effective method for personal growth. Lena specializes in harmonizing gratitude, conscious intention, and practical steps to offer a comprehensive approach to manifestation. As a highly sought-after coach, she inspires numerous individuals to overcome limiting beliefs and take control of their destinies. Contributing to the book "Plan the Life You Love," Lena shares insights on the power of gratitude, the art of visualization, and practical strategies to transform desires into extraordinary reality. Through her coaching and writing, Lena continues to make a positive impact, influencing others to align their thoughts and actions to their soul's purpose for a journey of abundance and fulfillment.

Plan A Life You Love...

IT'S A LIFESTYLE

A message from Lena...

Welcome to Your Manifestation Journey to the Life You Love!
Congratulations on taking the first step toward manifesting your dream. This journal is designed to be your companion on a 21-day adventure of intentional living. Each day, you'll find simple yet powerful prompts inspired by the key principles of manifestation. Whether you're new to the idea or looking to deepen your practice, these prompts are crafted to be accessible, practical, and, most importantly, tailored to your unique journey. Embrace each day with an open heart and a willingness to explore the potential within yourself. Manifestation is a personal and transformative process. Take your time, enjoy the journey, and celebrate the small victories along the way. You have the power to shape your reality into the Life You Love!

XOXO

LENA KHAIS - MANIFESTATION COACH AND AUTHOR IN PLAN A LIFE YOU LOVE

Picture Your Success:

Close your eyes and imagine yourself already having what you want. Feel how good it is. Write down your thoughts in this moment.

_____

_____

_____

_____

_____

_____

_____

_____

_____

_____

_____

_____

_____

_____

_____

_____

_____

_____

_____

_____

I am a magnet for financial abundance!

Say Positive Things:

Talk about your goals as if they're already happening. Use positive words.

_____
_____
_____
_____
_____
_____
_____
_____
_____
_____
_____
_____
_____
_____
_____
_____
_____
_____
_____

I am open to receiving wealth in expected and unexpected ways!

See the End Result:

Picture your life as if your dreams have already come true. Imagine it in detail. Describe it below.

I am worthy of the prosperity that comes into my life

Share to Receive:

Describe how you will give back when your goal is achieved. Exchange of energy is key.

_____
_____
_____
_____
_____
_____
_____
_____
_____
_____
_____
_____
_____
_____
_____
_____
_____
_____
_____
_____

I am grateful for the money flowing into my life

Speak with Confidence:

Talk about your goals like you believe in them. Use confident words.

I am attracting amazingn opportunities into my life

Feel Successful:

Imagine what it feels like to be successful. Feel it inside you. Write down your thoughts.

_____
_____
_____
_____
_____
_____
_____
_____
_____
_____
_____
_____
_____
_____
_____
_____
_____
_____
_____
_____

I am deserving of deep and fulfilling love

Make a Mental Movie:

Make a movie in your mind where everything goes the way you want it to. Write down the scenario.

_____

_____

_____

_____

_____

_____

_____

_____

_____

_____

_____

_____

_____

_____

_____

_____

_____

_____

_____

_____

_____

I am open to giving and receiving love in a healthy way

Talk in the Now:

Talk and think about your goals like they're happening right now.

_____

_____

_____

_____

_____

_____

_____

_____

_____

_____

_____

_____

_____

_____

_____

_____

_____

_____

_____

I am a magnet for positive and loving connections

Feel Good Inside:

Date: _____

Focus on feeling good inside. Be happy and positive. Write down your feelings.

_____
_____
_____
_____
_____
_____
_____
_____
_____
_____
_____
_____
_____
_____
_____
_____
_____
_____
_____

I am aligned with the energy of success and prosperity

Use a Symbol:

Choose something that reminds you of your goal. Keep it in your mind. Jot down moments when you see it.

_____
_____
_____
_____
_____
_____
_____
_____
_____
_____
_____
_____
_____
_____
_____
_____
_____
_____
_____

I am capable, competent, and ready for greatness

Imagine the Details:

Make your mental pictures detailed. Imagine all the little things. Write them down.

_____
_____
_____
_____
_____
_____
_____
_____
_____
_____
_____
_____
_____
_____
_____
_____
_____
_____

I am in control of my thoughts and focus on positive possibilities

Love Yourself:

_____

Tell yourself that you're important and deserving of good things. Write a love letter to yourself.

_____
_____
_____
_____
_____
_____
_____
_____
_____
_____
_____
_____
_____
_____
_____
_____
_____
_____
_____
_____
_____

I am creating a path of success that reflects my unique strengths and Talents

Kick Out Doubt:

Stop any thoughts that say you can't do it. Replace them with positive thoughts. Write them down.

_____
_____
_____
_____
_____
_____
_____
_____
_____
_____
_____
_____
_____
_____
_____
_____
_____

I am prepared and ready for success

Tell Your Mind at Night:

Before you sleep, tell yourself what you want. Your mind will listen. Write down your key points.

_____
_____
_____
_____
_____
_____
_____
_____
_____
_____
_____
_____
_____
_____
_____
_____
_____
_____
_____
_____
_____

I am attracting positive connections

Feel Your Power:

Know that you have the power to make things happen. Believe in yourself. Write down affirmations that make you feel powerful.

_____
_____
_____
_____
_____
_____
_____
_____
_____
_____
_____
_____
_____
_____
_____
_____
_____
_____
_____

I am worthy of a life that brings me both financial stability and personal satisfaction

Do Things That Help:

_____

Take actions that move you closer to your goals. Do things that make a difference. Write them down.

_____
_____
_____
_____
_____
_____
_____
_____
_____
_____
_____
_____
_____
_____
_____
_____
_____
_____
_____
_____

I am in tune with my body's needs

Let Go of Bad Feelings:

Forget about bad things from the past. Forgive and move on. Write them down. Now cross them out.

_____

_____

_____

_____

_____

_____

_____

_____

_____

_____

_____

_____

_____

_____

_____

_____

_____

I am grateful for the strength of my body and mind

Think Big:

Believe there's plenty for everyone, including you. Write your big thoughts.

I am surrounded by positive energy that contributes to my well-being

Trust Everything Will Work Out:

Believe that things will work out. Trust that everything is going to be okay. Write down situations that worked out in your favor.

_____

_____

_____

_____

_____

_____

_____

_____

_____

_____

_____

_____

_____

_____

_____

_____

_____

_____

_____

_____

I am creating a life filled with balance and well-being

Don't Worry, Believe:

Stop worrying. Believe in yourself and your dreams. Write down all great things that happened so far to get you closer to your goal.

_____

_____

_____

_____

_____

_____

_____

_____

_____

_____

_____

_____

_____

_____

_____

_____

_____

_____

_____

_____

_____

I am health and vitality in every aspect of my being

Spread Good Vibes:

Be positive and make others feel good. Positive energy attracts good things. Write down all your good deeds of today.

_____
_____
_____
_____
_____
_____
_____
_____
_____
_____
_____
_____
_____
_____
_____
_____
_____
_____
_____
_____

I am making conscious choices that support my overall wellness

Sylvia Becker-Hill

Becker-Hill Inc.
Inventor of Neuro Creativity®

https://www.linkedin.com/in/sylviabeckerhill/
https://www.facebook.com/SylviaBeckerHillBiz
https://www.instagram.com/sylviabeckerhill/
https://becker-hill.com
https://sylviabecker-hill.com

Sylvia Becker-Hill is a one-of-a-kind trailblazer in personal transformation and one of the matriarchs of the German coaching industry. Since 1997, she has served thousands of leaders worldwide as their executive coach and corporate leadership trainer. In 2002, she became the first German coach to be certified by the International Coach Federation as a Professional Certified Coach, and in 2023, one of the world's first ten Certified Master Neuroplasticians. As the inventor of the Neuro Creativity® framework, Sylvia blends science with soul to unlock the brain's capacity for deep healing and bold creation. An award-winning women's empowerment mentor, multiple times bestselling author, energetic edutainer, and soulscapes painting artist, she is a true Renaissance woman. Sylvia's mission is to empower you with all the knowledge and tools you need to "FLIP" everything that blocks, hurts, or frustrates you into unquestionable Freedom, unconditional Love, envisioned Identity, and impactful Power.

Plan A Life You Love...

IT'S YOUR PIECE OF ART YOU LEAVE BEHIND

A message from Sylvia...

I wrote many chapters for different anthologies over the past 22 years yet this one for Plan a Life You Love has a special place in my heart. Why? Because it is deeply personal and taught me a lot of things I wasn't aware of before I followed Hanna Oliva's invitation to contribute. Being an artist is not something I just do as a hobby or to make a living, it is a lifestyle, the embodiment of an archetype. My whole life is my masterpiece and each day is a new canvas. For me, life is never just black and white but rather extremely colorful. And even though I am a passionate academic erudite and scientist I don't just believe in magic: I know it is real. I designed this journal with the hope it will give you moments of joy in which you feel life's magic in your body. Let your colors flow...

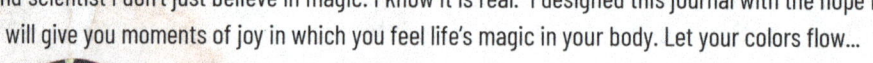

SYLVIA BECKER-HILL ARTIST & AUTHOR IN PLAN A LIFE YOU LOVE

Inner Compass Confidence™

How to FLIP from External Orientation to Being Guided by Soul

A Creative Exploration by Sylvia Becker-Hill

"Colors and images are the language of the Soul."

Welcome, Dear Reader of my chapter "Inner Compass Confidence"! To make the most out of the following journal pages that build upon my chapter in the anthology "Plan a Life You Love" you have ideally a pen and some colored pencils at hand.

Start by allowing yourself to relax your nervous system and to connect with your brilliant subconscious mind by using colors and drawing. Simply fill the compass below with the colors of your choice while gently contemplating your **understanding and definition of Inner Compass Confidence.**

"You are guided." Sylvia Becker-Hill

Reflections on Compass Confidence

1. Write down the results of your contemplation and how you feel after coloring the compass here into the lines and beyond if you need more space. Write also what you like or dislike about your insights and experience.

_____

_____

_____

_____

_____

2. Remember a time in your life, when you felt **'being without a compass'**, adrift, aimless... and when you remember that time, drop with your attention into your body and sense where do you feel that in your body and describe the sensation.

_____

_____

_____

_____

_____

"You are stronger than you think you are." Sylvia Becker-Hill

3. Remember a time in your life, when you felt **'being pulled by external forces'**, pushed, dragged, unable to escape external expectations and pressure… and when you remember that time, drop with your attention into your body and sense where you feel that and describe the sensation.

_____

_____

_____

_____

_____

4. Remember a time in your life, when you felt **'being guided by your internal compass'**, feeling confident, clear, trusting… and when you remember that time, drop your attention into your body and sense where you feel that and describe the sensation. (If you can't remember a time like that, don't worry, not many people can. If that's the case, IMAGINE how being guided by your inner compass might feel like and describe the matching sensations in your body.)

_____

_____

_____

_____

_____

"You matter. Without You there would be a hole in the universe." Sylvia Becker-Hill

Body Mapping Your Somatic Experiences

Look at your journaling from the two pages before and draw your 4 findings into the shape of the body below. Use different colors and different styles of pen strokes or patterns (dots, lines, swirls, stars... whatever feels intuitively fitting to express your feelings!) Feel the sensations you found in your body while giving them a form on paper! Feel the differences between the sensations and maybe take notes of any insights from this process.

"Your body loves you deeply." Sylvia Becker-Hill

External Orientation in Life

It's not about judging external orientation in life as wrong or right. It's about becoming conscious of how it shows up, which of our behaviors and patterns are a result of it and what the consequences are. Only you can decide:

Do you enjoy living "externally defined and pulled"?

Does it feel good and aligned with your heart's longing?

To become more conscious collect all the different external influences from the potential areas in your life over the next 2 pages. I added real personal examples from my own life and offer space for two additional areas you might have experienced.

Parents   *"Life is unfair. Be careful whom you trust."*

_____

_____

_____

_____

_____

Family   *"What will the neighbors think?!"*

_____

_____

_____

_____

Teachers   *"You are different and special."*

_____

_____

_____

_____

"Your are as unique as a snowflake." Sylvia Becker-Hill

Culture

"You have to be early or you're late!"

_____
_____
_____
_____
_____

Religion

"You are a sinner. Your body is a temptation for men."

_____
_____
_____
_____
_____

Technology

"I have to keep up and be online all the time or I'm out."

_____
_____
_____
_____

_____
_____
_____
_____

_____
_____
_____
_____

Connecting The Dots

The next step is about "connecting the dots" of your life. **Understanding how specific external drivers from your early childhood led to specific patterns of subconscious behavior** which you now can consciously embrace or let go of or adapt to your new circumstances as a mature adult.

I'll give you one example from my life and then you choose from the past 2 pages as any of your external influences you feel drawn to explore deeper.

External Influence	Coping Behavior	Keep/ Toss/ Adapt*
"What will the neighbors think?"	Pressure to confirm, strong anxiety, constant worry to be judged by others, a voice in my head commenting harshly everything I do.	Toss!

* Embracing life-long patterns is the easiest of the 3 options and brings peace. Tossing can be very hard but needed. Adaptation needs patience! A coach with expertise in applied neuroscience is a great resource to help with that!

"Just be you. The rest will follow." Sylvia Becker-Hill

Connecting The Dots Continued

External Influence	Coping Behavior	Keep/ Toss/ Adapt *
"Sweets are the reward for efforts."	"Eating unhealthy amounts of cakes and other sweets to relax after work."	Adapt: less plus alternatives

* Embracing life-long patterns is the easiest of the 3 options and brings **peace**. Tossing can be very hard but needed - like the one in my real example which I accomplished with EFT (Emotional Freedom Technique also known as "Tapping") after I discovered it in just one session because I'm a trained practitioner of this technique. Adaptation needs **patience**! A coach with expertise and tools in applied neuroscience is a great resource to help with that.

"Breath in lightness, breathe out heaviness." Sylvia Becker-Hill

Planning Power Awareness Questionnaire

Knowing ourselves and understanding how we function is crucial for **authentic embodied confidence** and for switching from external orientation to being internally guided by our soul.

I invite you to become conscious about your planning style, skills, and personality by going through the following Planning Power Awareness Questionnaire, which will indicate how you tend to approach planning in your life.

Write down your answers to the following questions as quickly as you can in the space provided:

1 How do you define planning?

2 Where do you think your definition of planning came from?

3 Describe the relationship you have with planning.

4 How does that relationship show up practically in your life?

5 How much do you plan?

6 In which areas of your life do you plan?

"Remember what you are: love and light!" Sylvia Becker-Hill

7 What is the time frame of your plans (weeks, months, or years)?

8 Describe the style of your planning, if you have one.

9 How much do you look at your plans, and how do you use them after they are made?

10 Have you been criticized by others for not planning at all, not enough, or not well enough? Or have you criticized yourself with your inner voice about your amount of planning? If yes, how did that make you feel?

11 How well has your way of planning worked for you? If not well, why do you think it didn't? If it works well, why do you think it worked?

"Do you hear the angels clapping? That's your applause." Sylvia Becker-Hill

60

12 Have you ever been traumatized by a plan going completely wrong? If yes, what effects did that experience have? How well have you recovered from it?

13 How confident are you regarding your planning skills?

14 Has your relationship with and/or style of planning changed over time?

15 How much do you use the following skills when planning? Write a percentage after the following skills (the total of all your percentages should add up to 100):

- Thinking
- Calculating
- Measuring
- Intuiting
- Sensing
- Feeling
- Aligning/releasing/healing in preparation
- Following external advice
- Using an existing/pre-fab plan
- Internal guidance/principles/beliefs

_____

100%

16 What did you discover? Did you have any realizations about how you approach planning?

"It's okay to relax." Sylvia Becker-Hill

The Three Planning Archetypes

In our book "Plan a Life You Love" I describe in my chapter the evolution of the three planning archetypes and how I perceive it. You will gain confidence to follow your own inner guidance when you **consciously own which traits of which archetype you already live and which you might want to develop.** (To fill the next two pages you might need to revisit the pages 74 till 80 top paragraph of the book.)

The Archetype of The Engeneer

I already live:

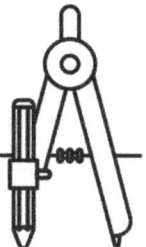

I plan to develop:

What I already created with those lived traits:

What I plan to created with those new traits:

"You are not your thoughts." Sylvia Becker-Hill

The Archetype of The Magic Tinkerbell

I already live:

I plan to develop:

What I already created with those lived traits:

What I plan to created with those new traits:

The Archetype of The Creative Artist

I already live:

I plan to develop:

What I already created with those lived traits:

What I plan to created with those new traits:

"You are not your emotions either." Sylvia Becker-Hill

The 5 Steps to a Magical Life

On pages 80 till 82 I talk about **the 5 practical steps** I took to plan and create my magical life. To remember them, write them into the stairs below. Do that slowly. Reread their description. Ensure you understand what I try to convey and if not, send me an email with your questions at: sylvia@becker-hill.com with the word "**compass**" in the subject line.

"From which star did you came from?" Sylvia Becker-Hill

Integration

To integrate all your journaling work and celebrate your progress and the invigorating magic of life, grab as many different colored markers as you have and enjoy a lovely time playing with these simple deliberately weak grey printed drawings over the next pages so you can adjust them to your liking and enjoy coloring them to your heart's desire and soul's joy! **Drawing over the lines is encouraged!** Capture any **insights or downloads from your Muse** while coloring in the lines below each image.

The Freedom to Curate Yourself *

*Before you start coloring this image, read page 80 again and focus on your answer to the question: "What am I?" from Step 1 of my 5 Steps to creating a life you love.

_____

_____

_____

Talk To The Moon About Your Dreams

"Your words are like magic spells. Use their power wisely." Sylvia Becker-Hill

Use Your Wishing Powers

———————————————————————————————

———————————————————————————————

———————————————————————————————

———————————————————————————————

———————————————————————————————

"Dance Darling! Dance!" Sylvia Becker-Hill

Collect Your Gained Strengths

Your self-awareness and strengths have grown over the time you worked through this journal. Capture them by writing them around this magic potion bottle and color them. Feel the somatic sensation of each strength while enjoying the creative expression of your growing Inner Compass Confidence!

Examples might be: Resilience, courage, patience, humor, creativity, curiosity...

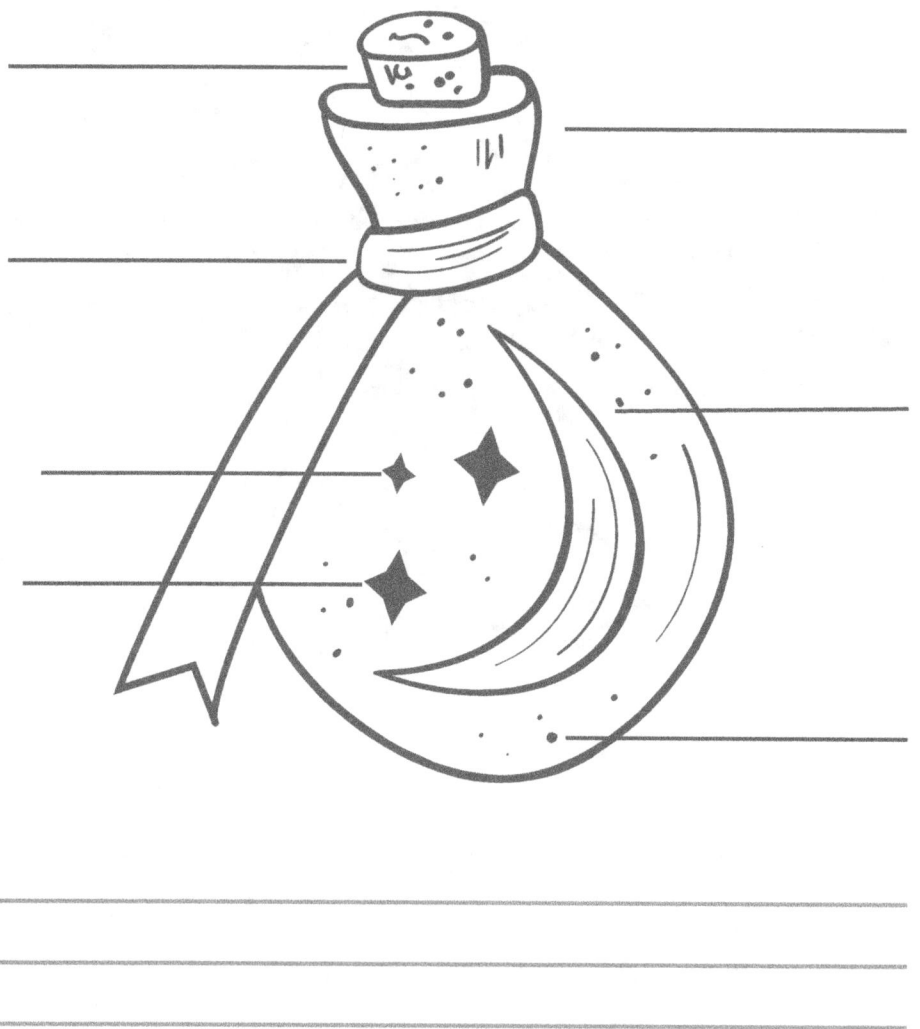

"Look at you Rock star!!!" Sylvia Becker-Hill

Draw a Vision of Your Embodied Future

People often make the mistake of worrying too much about specific external material details of their visions instead of focusing on their **embodiment of how they will feel once their dreams are realized**. Allow yourself to dream big and sense inside your body how you will feel when you **live with Inner Compass Confidence** and your strengths plus some "magic pixie dust". Write those words around the crystal ball and color it to express those feelings.

_____

_____

_____

"Oh! How perfect is that?!" Sylvia Becker-Hill

Celebrating the Arrival

You have arrived! Take a break, relax, and celebrate before you go to the next journal chapter. Look into your eyes in a mirror and see what has changed. Call a friend and talk about your growth and discoveries. I wish I could see your colorful pages... Maybe you like to share them as a photo in a review on Amazon. That would be a huge gift for me and my co-authors and triggers heaps of pixie dust from the universe!

xoxo,

Sylvia

"Stretch out your hand and touch the space that connects us all." Sylvia Becker-Hill

Prudence Hatchett

PH Counseling, LLC & Learn with Prudence
Mental Wellness Specialist

www.facebook.com/phcounselingllc
www.instagram.com/prudencehatchett
www.phcounseling.orglearn-with-prudence.myshopify.com

Prudence Hatchett is a best-selling author, business owner, licensed counselor, board certified coach, multi-endorsement educator, and multi-certified mental health professional. Prudence Hatchett earned a BA in Psychology and an M.S. in Special Education from Mississippi State University. She earned an M.Ed. in Counselor Education from the University of Mississippi. She owns a private practice, PH Counseling, LLC and ecommerce store and brand, Learn with Prudence. She has over 17 years of combined experience in the mental health and educational fields. She supports people in maturing their mental health and emotional wellness through the power of education, strength exploration, skill building, and elevating confidence.

Plan A Life You Love...

IT'S YOUR WINNING SEASON

A message from Prudence...

Did you notice all those smiling faces in my photo? This photo includes my mom, siblings, nieces, and nephews. This was taken after a championship win for the local high school girls basketball team, which my niece was a part of. This moment in time helped me remember that joy, excitement, and love are contagious, and they can spread like wildfire. Allow this book and journal to spark a fire within you. When you read the pages and participate in the journal prompts, I want you to feel the joy, excitement, and love that has been poured out into these pages just for you. The journey to discovering the life you love is full of wonder, appreciation, and manifestation of the life you deserve. By being an active participant in the discovery process, I learned to embrace my truest self without any reservations. And that is what I want for you. I want you to love your life. I want you to reconnect with your authentic self so you can plan a life you love. My chapter is all about the discovery process and removing the barriers that are standing in your way. The time is now for you to start your winning season, and I am here to celebrate with you!

PRUDENCE HATCHETT- THE JOURNEY TO DISCOVERING THE LIFE YOU LOVE

The Miracle Question:

Imagine waking up today and all your doubts, fears, & obstacles have disappeared. You now have magical powers to create and manifest anything you want in your life. Now, describe this life with as many details as you can.

I Am Magical

73

Take a moment to reflect on your current life:

_____

Describe how your current life differs from your miracle life you described. Describe what is similar.

_____
_____
_____
_____
_____
_____
_____
_____
_____
_____
_____
_____
_____
_____
_____
_____
_____
_____
_____
_____

I Can Create Miracles

"I am capable of embracing my life's journey toward creating a life I love"

Date:

_____

Write this affirmation 10 times below:

_____

_____

_____

_____

_____

_____

_____

_____

_____

_____

_____

_____

_____

_____

_____

_____

_____

_____

_____

_____

I Am Capable

Let's have fun:

List 20 things you love. This can include things, places, objects, activities. Rule: can't include people.

_____

_____

_____

_____

_____

_____

_____

_____

_____

_____

_____

_____

_____

_____

_____

_____

_____

_____

_____

_____

_____

I Am Loving

Identify Barriers:

What barriers are standing in the way of you planning a life you love?

_____

_____

_____

_____

_____

_____

_____

_____

_____

_____

_____

_____

_____

_____

_____

_____

_____

_____

I Can Remove Barriers

Self-awareness

Describe your definition of self-awareness. Are you self-aware according to your own definition?

_____

_____

_____

_____

_____

_____

_____

_____

_____

_____

_____

_____

_____

_____

_____

_____

_____

_____

I Am Self-aware

Reflect on your Talents:

Describe at least 10 talents (or strengths) you have.

_____
_____
_____
_____
_____
_____
_____
_____
_____
_____
_____
_____
_____
_____
_____
_____
_____
_____
_____
_____

I Am Talented

Dream Job:

Describe your dream job. How does it compare to the one you have now (if applicable).

_____

_____

_____

_____

_____

_____

_____

_____

_____

_____

_____

_____

_____

_____

_____

_____

_____

_____

_____

_____

I Am A Dreamer

Life Changes:

How has your life changed over the last two year?

_____

_____

_____

_____

_____

_____

_____

_____

_____

_____

_____

_____

_____

_____

_____

_____

_____

_____

_____

_____

I Am Changing

Life Changes cont.

Are you afraid of changes? What has been your most scariest change? What has been your most positive change?

_____
_____
_____
_____
_____
_____
_____
_____
_____
_____
_____
_____
_____
_____
_____
_____
_____
_____

I Can Change

Life Changes cont.

Imagine its 5 years from now, what do you want to look back at this moment and say about yourself?

_____

_____

_____

_____

_____

_____

_____

_____

_____

_____

_____

_____

_____

_____

_____

_____

_____

_____

_____

I Can Change My Life

Reflecting on Emotions:

What helps you feel comfortable, calm, and grounded?

_____
_____
_____
_____
_____
_____
_____
_____
_____
_____
_____
_____
_____
_____
_____
_____
_____

I Feel Comforted

Reflecting on Emotions:

What makes you feel anxious and fearful?

_____

_____

_____

_____

_____

_____

_____

_____

_____

_____

_____

_____

_____

_____

_____

_____

_____

I Can Manage My Anxiety

Reflecting on Emotions:

Describe the moments when you felt the most confident and proud of yourself?

_____

_____

_____

_____

_____

_____

_____

_____

_____

_____

_____

_____

_____

_____

_____

_____

_____

I Feel Proud

Personal Needs:

What are your most 5 pressing needs at the moment? Describe how you felt answering this.

_____

_____

_____

_____

_____

_____

_____

_____

_____

_____

_____

_____

_____

_____

_____

_____

_____

_____

_____

I Am In This Moment

Goal Setting:

What goals do you need to make in order to fulfill your needs?

_____
_____
_____
_____
_____
_____
_____
_____
_____
_____
_____
_____
_____
_____
_____
_____
_____
_____

I Am A Goal-Setter

Gratitude:

_____

List 10 things you are grateful for.

_____

_____

_____

_____

_____

_____

_____

_____

_____

_____

_____

_____

_____

_____

_____

_____

_____

_____

I Am Grateful

Embrace:

What do you need to embrace about yourself?

_____
_____
_____
_____
_____
_____
_____
_____
_____
_____
_____
_____
_____
_____
_____
_____
_____
_____
_____

I Can Embrace Me

Letting Go:

What do you need to let go of to plan a life you love?

_____

_____

_____

_____

_____

_____

_____

_____

_____

_____

_____

_____

_____

_____

_____

_____

I Can Let Go

I Am Ready:

What life signs points to you being ready to plane a life you love?

I Am Ready

Year in Review for Planning a Life You Love!:

Date:

_____

What do you want your life to look like a year from now? What do you need to do today that will make that a reality?

_____

_____

_____

_____

_____

_____

_____

_____

_____

_____

_____

_____

_____

_____

_____

_____

_____

_____

_____

I Can Plan A Life I Love

Trish Gleason

The World Wellness Show, LLC
Host and CEO

https://www.linkedin.com/in/lovetaxfree
https://www.facebook.com/loveworldwellness
https://www.instagram.com/lovetaxfree
https://www.worldwellnessinterviews.com/
https://www.youtube.com/@theworldwellnessshow

Trish Gleason is a dedicated host and the founder of The World Wellness Show, LLC, a streaming TV Show now broadcasting in 137 countries on FENIX TV, a platform committed to sharing educational health and wellness information through insightful interviews with holistic doctors and other specialists. Born and raised in the Midwest USA, Trish has always had a profound passion for helping and educating others.

With a successful career as a wealth advisor spanning 29 years, Trish's path took an additional direction when she discovered a deep interest in the holistic methodologies practiced by many of her doctor clients. This newfound passion led her to launch her own TV show in 2018, where she has been engaging in conversations with medical professionals to spread awareness and knowledge about holistic health practices.

Beyond her professional endeavors, Trish is a loving grandmother to fifteen-grandchildren and proud mother of three children. Her dedication to making a positive impact by creating a paradigm shift from sick care to wellcare shines through everything she does.

Plan A Life You Love...
READY, SET, REVERSE!

A message from Trish...

Welcome to Your Journey of Intentional Living

In this companion journal to the international best-seller Plan a Life You Love, I invite you to take a proactive step toward your health, wellness, and overall joy. My chapter, Ready, Set, Reverse, was inspired by interviews with world-renowned doctors on The World Wellness Show, where I serve as host. Through their groundbreaking insights and the wisdom, I've gathered, I've shared practical strategies for reversing the effects of stress, aging, and imbalance—starting from within. This journal is your sacred space to manifest a life filled with vitality, clarity, and purpose. Let it guide you as you reflect, dream, and design a life you truly love—one healthy, empowered step at a time.

TRISH GLEASON - HOST OF THE WORLD WELLNESS SHOW, LLC

Ready, Set, Reverse!

New Discoveries That Turn Back the Clock of Aging

- You enjoyed some fabulous material as you read the women's self-help book Plan a Life You Love!

- You became energized to make some changes to improve and plan your life!

- Finally, unfortunately you will FORGET MOST EVERYTHING within a few short weeks!

Unless you REACT & start a plan NOW nothing will happen because fewer than 5% of readers utilize even one suggestion from a book. Make a difference in your life. This journal is to help you make something happen, create your notes about areas which apply to you and document notes for your continued research. It would be impractical for you to spend hundreds of hours researching and interviewing some of the world's most recognized holistic doctors to learn new and powerful technologies to empower you to live longer, healthier, more energetic and youthful. Great news! As you know, nine authors and I have done part of the work for you in the book Plan a Life You Love. Let's take advantage and get busy to help you plan for a more wonderful life.

_____

_____

_____

_____

_____

_____

_____

_____

_____

_____

_____

You've read the book—now make it real

Identify Your Needs - Your Goals --

Whether your goal is to reverse an illness, prevent an illness, have more energy or have an age defying objective or something else let's identify your need(s). For example, my need is.

"To be aware of and apply modern biohacking, therapies and other technologies that are holistic to help me have more energy, have a youthful appearance and live a very long time."

Here are a few suggestions to document your specific need(s):

- I have an illness I want to reverse.

- I want to be proactive and prevent illness by learning about and applying holistic and other wellness strategies.

- I have a loved one I want to help become healthier.

- I am overall not healthy, eating poorly and just not aware of what is good for me, so I want to learn.

- I have hormonal issues and need guidance.

- I eat poorly and feel tired all the time.

- I am depressed from time to time and have a difficult time going out.

- I get dizzy sometimes and do not know how to overcome it.

- I am overweight and want to slim down.

Clear needs create clear steps forward.

Identify Your Needs - Your Goals --

Date:

_____

_____

_____

_____

_____

_____

_____

_____

_____

_____

_____

_____

_____

_____

_____

_____

_____

_____

_____

_____

_____

_____

_____

_____

Clear needs create clear steps forward.

Life Expectancy

What is your Life Expectancy? The average life expectancy for people in the US is 78.9 years as of 2024. By creating a paradigm shift for yourself changing from sick care to a pre-sickness mindset involving well care you most likely will add years to your lifespan. Share this information with your loved ones.

_____

_____

_____

_____

_____

_____

_____

_____

_____

_____

_____

_____

_____

_____

_____

_____

_____

_____

_____

Your Life Is a Garden— Tend to It Early.

General Information

Age
_____

Date:
_____

Biological/Epigenetic Clock vs Chronological Age

Date:
_____

Understanding the new technologies and knowledge available today can reverse your lifespan creating a much younger BIOLOGICAL AGE. Biological age is based on how old your cells are. As your cells age, they lose their ability to regenerate and repair themselves. Stress and genetics can trigger senescence (lose ability to regenerate) in your cells.

_____

_____

_____

_____

_____

_____

_____

_____

_____

_____

_____

_____

_____

Reclaim Your Youth From the Inside Out.

Purpose

Purpose in your life can influence physical health, influence physical health to live longer, protect against heart disease, prevent Alzheimer's disease, handle pain better and lead to better relationships according to the University of Minnesota's research. Do you know what your purpose is? Discover what it is and document it here? You could have more than one purpose.

For example, my purpose is to promote health, wellness, and anti-aging to the world and to enjoy my family. Your purpose could be: Traveling and exploring different cultures, supporting the Cancer Society, being on the board and active in a Women's Club, your job (I've heard if you love your job, it is not a job), to be a Girl Scout Leader, to embrace being a mother with children you are raising.

_____

_____

_____

_____

_____

_____

_____

_____

_____

_____

_____

Purpose is Your Inner Compass

3 - Steps Homework

 # 1 - Make a commitment to watch the following Netflix documentaries. You may think you don't want to watch scientific and slow-going programs but believe me you will have a difficult time getting up from your seat. Once you watch them check the boxes below then share with your loved ones.

☐ Live to 100: Secrets of the Blue Zones _____

_____

_____

_____

☐ You Are What You Eat – A Twin Experiment _____

_____

_____

_____

☐ What The Health _____

_____

_____

_____

_____

☐ Poisoned, The Dirty Truth About Food _____

_____

_____

_____

_____

Hit Play on a New Perspective

3 - Steps Homework

#2 – In 2018 I started a FB Group called HUSHLadies where women could post their secrets passed on by their mothers and grandmothers. Educational only – non selling. People either post or message me to post their secrets. Go to this free group and scan through the posts to pick up some fantastic solutions. In the Helan period from the year 794 to 1185 women in Japan's royal court dawned hair that flowed to the ground. Their secret was fermented rice water.

Listed below are just a few of the topics. Checkmark the topics you would like to learn more about and head on over to the group to investigate – it's free.

- [ ] Red Light Therapy and Healing
- [ ] Micro Exfoliants
- [ ] Hyaluronic Acid Serum
- [ ] Halo Treatment
- [ ] Snail Mucus Pads
- [ ] 75 Names for Sugar
- [ ] Scalp Scrub
- [ ] Seasonal Hair Loss
- [ ] Fermented Rice Water for Hair Growth
- [ ] Reversing Hunchback Stretch
- [ ] Hormonal Imbalance
- [ ] Flaxseed and Hair Growth
- [ ] Omega 3 Fat
- [ ] Alzheimer's Potential Reversal
- [ ] Microcurrent Biofeedback Technology
- [ ] Niacinamide
- [ ] Epley Maneuver for Dizziness
- [ ] Gua Sha and Microcurrents for Facial Lymphatic Cleansing

Tap Into Generations of Wisdom

3-Steps Homework

#2 - In 2018 I started a FB Group called HUSHladies where women could post their secrets passed on by their mothers and grandmothers. Educational only – non selling. People either post or message me to post their secrets. Go to this free group and scan through the posts to pick up some fantastic solutions. In the Helan period from the year 794 to 1185 women in Japan's royal court dawned hair that flowed to the ground. Their secret was fermented rice water.

Notes:

_____

_____

_____

_____

_____

_____

_____

_____

_____

_____

_____

_____

_____

_____

_____

_____

_____

Tap Into Generations of Wisdom

3-Steps Homework

#3 - FENIXtv.app - Go to the FENIXtv app, which is downloadable from any smart TV for free. The download is free and the viewing/membership is free. So many great programs are available to empower women or really anybody. The topics range from financial planning to mental health and beyond. Document the free programs you want to watch on https://fenixtv.app/

_____

_____

_____

_____

_____

_____

_____

_____

_____

_____

_____

_____

_____

_____

_____

_____

_____

_____

Fuel Your Growth—For Free

Quiz

What is regenerative medicine?

A. The process of replacing or "regenerating" human cells.

B. Replace tissue or organs that have been damaged by age, disease, trauma, or congenital issues.

C. Engineer, regenerate or replace tissue using natural growth and repair mechanisms such as stem cells. Organoids, 3D organ printing, and tissue engineering are examples of bio powered technologies used in some therapies.

Notes _____

_____

_____

_____

_____

_____

_____

_____

_____

_____

_____

_____

Answer: (All)

Knowledge is Power—Let's Begin

Quiz

What part of the body is considered your "second brain"?

A. Your Heart

B. Your Lungs

C. Your Belly

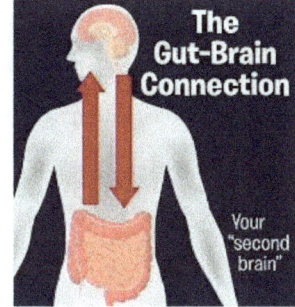

Notes _____

_____

_____

_____

_____

_____

_____

_____

_____

(Answer: YOUR BELLY/GUT) Hopkinsmedicine.org explains "If you've ever "gone with your gut" to decide something or felt "butterflies in your stomach" when nervous, you're likely getting signals from an unexpected source: your second brain." Your second brain is directly linked to

Knowledge is Power—Let's Begin

Quiz

Date:

_____

What is Biohacking?

A. The use of sleep tracking devices. The wearing of blue light-blocking glasses. Light therapy for circadian rhythm regulation.

B. Wearing a FitBit

C. Meditation

Notes _____

_____

_____

_____

_____

_____

_____

_____

_____

_____

_____

_____

_____

Answer: (ALL)

Knowledge is Power—Let's Begin

Food I Eat

Date:

_____

Brain – Gut, Gut – Brain Connection. Now that we know your GUT is your second brain let's find out what you're fueling your brain with. What do you consume? Be honest. When you make a virtual call with a holistic specialist they will ask you. Check each of the following you consume then add other foods in the space below.

- [ ] Eggs
- [ ] Beef, Pork, Chicken (antibiotic free or not)
- [ ] Soda
- [ ] Chocolate
- [ ] Vegetables/Fruit
- [ ] Oatmeal
- [ ] Legumes
- [ ] Yogurt (sweetened/unsweetened)
- [ ] Bran Muffins
- [ ] Sushi
- [ ] Fruit Snacks Like Fruit Roll-Ups
- [ ] Hazelnut – Chocolate Spread
- [ ] Baked Veggie Chip Snacks
- [ ] Granola Bars
- [ ] Pretzels
- [ ] Bacon
- [ ] Lunch Meat
- [ ] Cow's Milk

What fuels you fuels your brain. Check what you eat

Food I Eat

_____

Notes _____

_____

_____

_____

_____

_____

_____

_____

_____

_____

_____

_____

_____

_____

_____

_____

_____

Tap Into Generations of Wisdom

Author's Key Takeaways

Checkmark the suggestions you will implement.

☐ <u>Delta Sleep</u>. Fall asleep with a clear mind and do not lay your head on the pillow and crash. Breathe, sort out the day and put the issues in the back of your mind. As Dr. Patrick Porter of Brain Tap Technologies explained how getting into DELTA SLEEP is imperative for your brain to create more neurotransmitters. Serotonin is a neurotransmitter. Most is produced by and found in the intestine (approximately 90%), and the remainder in <u>central nervous system</u> neurons. It functions to regulate appetite, sleep, memory and learning, temperature, mood, behavior, muscle contraction, and function of the <u>cardiovascular system</u> and <u>endocrine system</u>. Wikipedia. During the interview Dr. Porter suggested eliminating watching the news as a way to keep your mind clear at night.

Notes _____

_____

_____

_____

_____

_____

_____

_____

_____

_____

_____

Turn insight into action

Author's Key Takeaways

☐ _Intermittent Fasting_. Want to extend your longevity? Intermittent fasting likely will put you in the right direction. Allowing the food to digest by only eating in 6 - 8 hour periods allows the food time to digest and creates a more efficient body with most likely a longer lifespan. Choices about sleep patterns, diet and exercise can have a tremendous effect on our level of wellness. - Dr. Stephen Anton

Notes _____

_____

_____

_____

_____

☐ _Fascia_. Dr. Daniel Fenster is an authority on the body's fascia and describes how it connects to every organ in the body. Waking up after 7 - 9 hours your body is dehydrated. Keep a glass of water next to you and drink a full 8 ounces upon waking to rehydrate your body and nourish your fascia. Fascia is a thin casing of connective tissue that surrounds and holds every organ, blood vessel, bone, nerve fiber and muscle in place. The tissue does more than provide internal structure, fascia has nerves that make it almost as sensitive as skin.

Notes _____

_____

_____

_____

_____

Turn insight into action

Author's Key Takeaways

☐ <u>Gut-Brain Relationship</u>. Dr. Lankering helped us understand how the gut is your 2nd brain and even produces more serotonin than the brain. Serotonin (a neurotransmitter) or 5-hydroxytryptamine is a monoamine neurotransmitter. Its biological function is complex, touching on diverse functions including mood, cognition, reward, learning, memory, and numerous physiological processes such as vomiting and vasoconstriction. <u>Wikipedia</u> A way to create more serotonin, as Dr. Lankering explained, is to chew your food completely, eat a more plant based diet, consume non GMO foods and eat raw foods as cooked plants do not have or have little digestive enzymes.

Notes _____

_____

_____

_____

☐ <u>Stress Causing 90% of Illness</u>. Dr. Clint Steele helped us understand our brains cannot be in healing mode and survival mode at the same time. If your brain's "norm" is stuck in survival mode you are not able to heal. Thanks to neuroplasticity, these patterns can be changes leading to a longer, healthier life. Neuroplasticity is the brain's ability to change and adapt due to experience. It is an umbrella term referring to the brain's ability to change, reorganize, or grow neural networks. This can involve functional changes due to brain damage or structural changes due to learning. If your brain is not in healing mode it will drastically effect your digestion of food, sleep, reproduction, blood pressure, inflammation, pain, anxiety and just about everything.

Notes _____

_____

_____

_____

Turn insight into action

Author's Key Takeaways

☐ <u>Regenerative Stem Cell Therapy</u>. Babies have 1 in 10k stem cells, while in a 60-year-old, this number decreases to 1 in 10 million. Stem cells divide into skin, liver and more and are crucial in the body's repair and regeneration processes. explained by Dr. Paul Finucan of Naples, Florida. What can you do to regenerate and create more stem cells? Dr Finucan suggests searching on Google your specific disorder or injury followed by the word "exosomes" or "stem cells". Check the areas you want to further research.

Enhanced Stimulation of Targeted Areas

- Inject Wharton's Jelly
- Stem Cell Therapy
- Stem Cell Treatments
- Red Light Therapy
- Arthritis

Notes _____

_____

_____

_____

_____

_____

_____

_____

Turn insight into action

Where Can I Get Answers and Help?

Dr. Steven Anton – Intermittent Fasting & Longevity (+001.1.352.273.7514)

Notes _____
_____
_____

Dr. Paul Finucan – Hormones & Stem Cell Therapy (drfinucan@gmail.com)

Notes _____
_____
_____

Dr. Tom Lankering – The Gut/The 2nd Brain and Longevity (dradjust@sopris.net)

Notes _____
_____
_____

Dr. Clint Steele – 90% of Disease Due To Stress/Brain Based Health (brainbasedhs.com)

Notes _____
_____
_____

You don't have to figure it out alone.

Where Can I Get Answers and Help?

Dr. Patrick Porter - Sleep Expert/Sleep is Crucial to Longevity (heidi@braintap.com)

Notes _____

_____

_____

Dr. Daniel Fenster - Fascia Connects All Organs & Pain Solutions (dr.fenster@completewellnessnyc.com)

Notes _____

_____

_____

You don't have to figure it out alone.

Resources

Body Mass Index Calculator. https://www.forbes.com/health/wellness/bmi-calculator/

Blood Sugar Answers. https://www.forbes.com/health/wellness/normal-blood-sugar-levels/

Blood Oxygen Answers. https://www.forbes.com/health/wellness/normal-blood-oxygen-levels/

Biological Age Testing. Some of the most respected biological age tests are epigenetic clocks, sometimes called DNA methylation tests. Other clocks incorporate external factors like smoking history, or chronological age into a biological age calculation. myDNAge® biological age test, is based on Dr. Horvath's epigenetic age clock. Newer tests based on DNA methylation appear to better measure aging. DNA methylation is a reversible biological process that controls gene expression but doesn't alter underlying DNA. Methylation patterns become more random with age.

Feel free to reach out to me with questions or possibly I can direct you to a specialist if needed. We are happy you are going on this inspiring journey of self-discovery, exploring the transformative power of a proactive approach to health, wellness and anti-aging. Please email me with the changes in your health while using the holistic technologies as mentioned in this chapter.

Trish Gleason
Gainesville Florida.
352.871.7171 or 404.444.0905.
help@theworldwellnessshow.com

THE WORLD
WELLNESS
Show

A Life You Love Starts Now

So here you are, pen in hand, heart wide open.
You've taken the first step toward something extraordinary: yourself.
This journal was never just about plans or prompts. It's about power. Yours.
To design a life that honors your dreams.
To pursue health, wealth, and happiness without apology or permission.
To make room for your evolution: messy, beautiful, and real.

You've explored your intentions, your purpose, your possibilities.
Now, keep going. Keep choosing you.
Let every page you fill be a vote for the life you deserve.
Let every goal you set be a bold refusal to shrink.
Let every reflection be proof that you are growing, healing, rising.

This is not the end.
This is you. Rewriting your story, one powerful, intentional page at a time.
And the best part?
You're just getting started.

HANNA OLIVAS

JOIN THE MOVEMENT!
#BAUW
Becoming An Unstoppable Woman
With She Rises Studios

She Rises Studios was founded by Hanna Olivas and Adriana Luna Carlos, the mother-daughter duo, in mid-2020 as they saw a need to help empower women worldwide. They are the podcast hosts of the *She Rises Studios Podcast* and Amazon best-selling authors and motivational speakers who travel the world. Hanna and Adriana are the movement creators of #BAUW - Becoming An Unstoppable Woman: The movement has been created to universally impact women of all ages, at whatever stage of life, to overcome insecurities, and adversities, and develop an unstoppable mindset. She Rises Studios educates, celebrates, and empowers women globally.

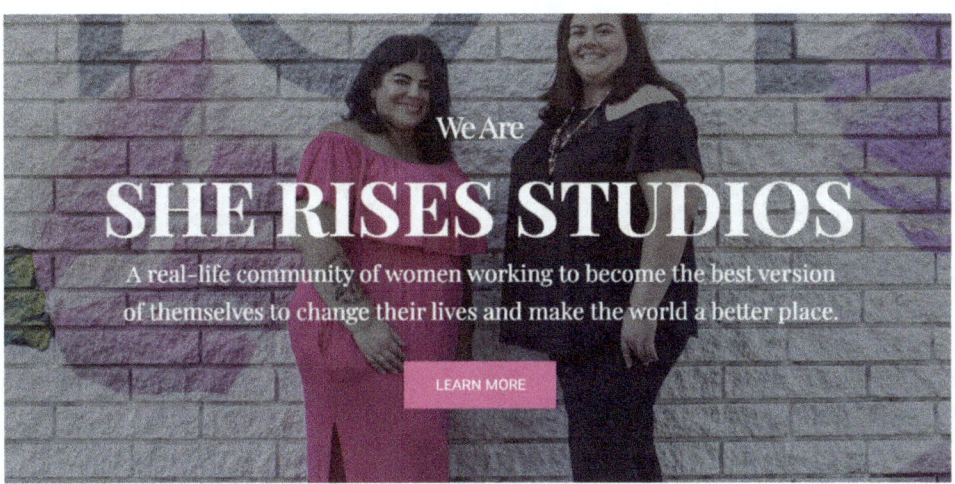

Looking to Join Us in our Next Anthology or Publish YOUR Own?

She Rises Studios Publishing offers full-service publishing, marketing, book tour, and campaign services. For more information, contact info@sherisesstudios.com

We are always looking for women who want to share their stories and expertise and feature their businesses on our podcasts, in our books, and in our magazines.

SEE WHAT WE DO

OUR PODCAST

OUR BOOKS

OUR SERVICES

Be featured in the Becoming An Unstoppable Woman magazine, published in 13 countries and sold in all major retailers. Get the visibility you need to LEVEL UP in your business!

 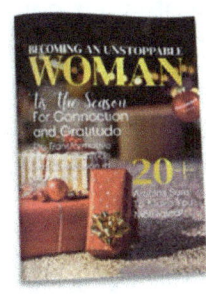 

Have your own TV show streamed across major platforms like Roku TV, Amazon Fire Stick, Apple TV and more!

Learn to leverage your expertise. Build your online presence and grow your audience with FENIX TV.
https://fenixtv.sherisesstudios.com/

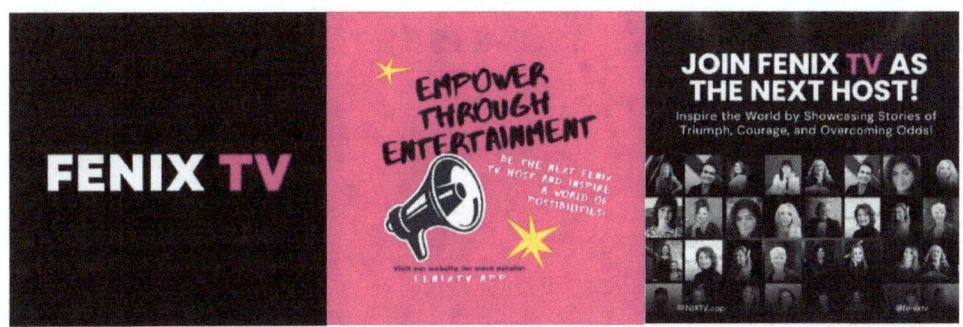

Visit www.SheRisesStudios.com to see how YOU can join the #BAUW movement and help your community to achieve the UNSTOPPABLE mindset.

Have you checked out the *She Rises Studios Podcast?*

Find us on all MAJOR platforms: Spotify, IHeartRadio, Apple Podcasts, Google Podcasts, etc.

Looking to become a sponsor or build a partnership?

Email us at info@sherisesstudios.com

SHE RISES
S T U D I O S